Transportation & Communication Series

All About
Sign Language

Talking With Your Hands

Felicia Lowenstein

Enslow Publishers, Inc.

40 Industrial Road   PO Box 38
Box 398   Aldershot
Berkeley Heights, NJ 07922 Hants GU12 6BP
USA   UK

http://www.enslow.com

*The editor would like to thank Catherine Valcourt-Pearce
and Dennis Berrigan of Gallaudet University's Laurent Clerc National Deaf
Education Center for their guidance.*

Copyright © 2004 by Enslow Publishers, Inc.

Library of Congress Cataloging-in-Publication Data

Lowenstein, Felicia.
   All about sign language : talking with your hands / Felicia Lowenstein.
      v. cm. — (Transportation & communication series)
   Includes bibliographical references and index.
   Contents: The unspoken language—Signs of the times—The history of sign language—People who sign—Jobs with sign language—The future of sign language.
   ISBN 0-7660-2028-2
   1. Sign language—Juvenile literature. 2. Sign language—History—Juvenile literature. [1. Sign language.]
I. Title. II. Series.
HV2476.L69 2004
419—dc22

                                   2003026608

Printed in the United States of America

10 9 8 7 6 5 4 3 2

Illustration Credits: © 1996–2003 ArtToday.com, Inc., pp. 2, 29; © 1999 Artville, LLC., p. 28; Associated Press, pp. 1, 6, 7, 9, 20–21, 24, 32, 33, 34, 37, 38, 40 (top and bottom); Associated Press, The Morning Journal, p. 10; Corel Corporation, pp. 26 (background), 27; Dover Publications, Inc., pp. 17 (bottom), 23; Enslow Publishers, Inc., pp. 11, 12, 13, 39; Gallaudet University Archives, pp. 17 (top), 18, 19, 26 (inset), 31, 36; Courtesy of Helen Keller Property Board, Tuscumbia, Alabama, pp. 4, 8; Hemera Technologies, Inc. 1997–2000, pp. 5, 14, 16, 45; Library of Congress, p. 30; Courtesy of the Martha's Vineyard Historical Society, p. 22; Painet Inc., pp. 15, 25, 35, 41.

Cover Illustration: Enslow Publishers, Inc.

Contents

Chapter 1

The Unspoken Language

C A K E

C-A-K-E. The strange fingershapes made no sense to seven-year-old Helen Keller. She grabbed the cake her teacher offered. She had no idea she spelled the word to earn it.

A long time ago, Helen could hear, see, and even say some words. She was nearly two years old when she became very sick. The doctors did not think she would live. She did, but she could not see or hear.

Helen's parents were afraid for their daughter. In 1887, people who were blind and deaf almost never learned to read or write. Sometimes they learned simple jobs.

Helen Keller (left) became famous for what she learned. She helped others.

Helen Keller (left), at age thirteen, learned how to communicate with the help of Anne Sullivan (right).

Something had to be done, but how could they reach Helen? She was growing wild.

That is when Helen's parents hired a teacher, Anne Sullivan. She began by trying to teach Helen basic handshapes for letters of the alphabet. Because Helen was blind, Sullivan spelled them into her hands.

In fact, Sullivan spelled into Helen's hands everything the two did all day long. For a month, Helen repeated the fingerspelling. She thought it was a game.

Then suddenly it became more than a game. It was a warm spring morning that April 3, 1887. Sullivan was having trouble showing Helen the difference between *milk*, *mug*, and *drink*.

Then Sullivan had an idea. She took Helen

outside to the water pump. Sullivan pumped while Helen held her mug up to fill it. As the cold water hit her hand, Helen seemed surprised. Her face changed.

She remembered. One of the first words Helen had said as a baby was "wa-wa" for

In 1953, Helen Keller (center) met President Dwight D. Eisenhower. Keller's friend, Polly Thomson, fingerspelled to Keller what the president said.

Anne Sullivan took Helen Keller outside to the water pump. One of the first words Helen learned was W-A-T-E-R.

water. "I knew that W-A-T-E-R meant the wonderful cool something that was flowing over my hand," she said years later when retelling the event.

With hands still wet, Helen dropped to her knees. She touched her hands to the ground. "What is this?" she seemed to say. Sullivan quickly spelled it for her. Helen then asked for the name of the pump. Finally she put her hand on Sullivan. What was she called?

Sullivan spelled the word T-E-A-C-H-E-R. It was what Helen would call her the rest of their lives.

That morning, Helen Keller discovered a new way to communicate. It was fingerspelling, also called the manual alphabet.

Manual alphabets and handshapes are used together to become sign language.

Chapter 2

Signs of the Times

An important part of signing is where and how your hands are positioned.

Sign language is communicating with your hands. It is not as simple as just holding up your hand. There are signs for words and ideas. You need to learn these signs in order to communicate using sign language.

Each sign is made up of four parts. They are handshape, hand movement, location, and position of the palm. The looks you make with your face while signing are also very important.

Let us start with handshape. This means the position of the hand. Where are the fingers? How is the hand bent?

These kids are signing
a holiday song.

Try the handshape for *I love you*. Hold your hand palm facing out. Keep your thumb, pinky, and index fingers up. Fold the other two down. You have just made a sign. You can show it to your friends and family.

I LOVE YOU

The second part of a sign is hand movement. Take the *I love you* sign. Instead of holding it palm out, turn your palm down. Then move your hand out and away from you two times. You have just signed the word *airplane*.

AIRPLANE

Maybe you want to say instead that you were flying in an airplane. Make the airplane sign once, instead of twice. Move it farther away from your body. You can see how you have to pay close attention to both handshapes and movements to understand what someone is signing.

FATHER

MOTHER

FINE

Another important part of a sign is where you are holding your hands. Are they at chest level? Near your stomach? Near your head or neck? Where the sign is made can also change its meaning.

Open your hand so it is flat with your fingers spread apart. Tap your thumb to the side of your forehead twice. You have just signed *father*. Signs for men are often made at the forehead. This could be because men used to wear fancy hats.

Now hold your hand the same way. Move it down by the side of your chin and tap your thumb on your chin twice. You have just signed *mother*.

Try one more. Keep your hand the same way. Touch the center of your chest with your thumb. You have just signed *fine*.

Finally, look at your palm. In sign

language, it can be up or down, right or left. Each direction changes the meaning.

Now try this sign. Cup your hands together as if you are making a hamburger patty. Then switch your hands and repeat the motion. You have just signed *hamburger*.

Now cup your hands together once. You just signed *wife*. Learn the signs exactly. Or you might just say *hamburger* when you mean *wife*!

Many people learn the American Manual Alphabet in addition to American Sign Language (ASL). It contains twenty-six handshapes, one for each letter of the English alphabet. You might use fingerspelling for someone's name or a sign you do not know.

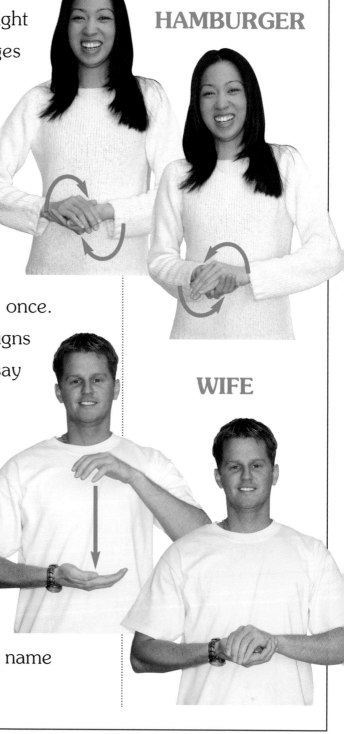

HAMBURGER

WIFE

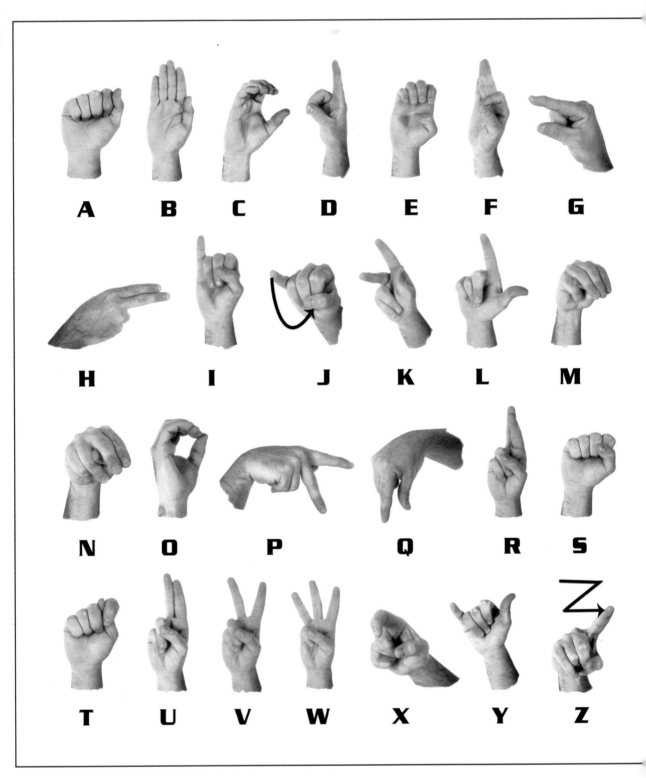

A B C D E F G

H I J K L M

N O P Q R S

T U V W X Y Z

Within the deaf culture, there are many types of sign language. Sign language is also used all over the world.

See an example of a manual alphabet on page 14. Practice making the letter shapes with your hands. Notice which shapes look like the letters themselves.

Within the deaf culture there are many different ways of signing. Sign language is used all over the world. You may think ASL is English but it is not. ASL uses a different grammar, or order of words, than English. You can sign in English but it is not ASL. Each language has its own sign language.

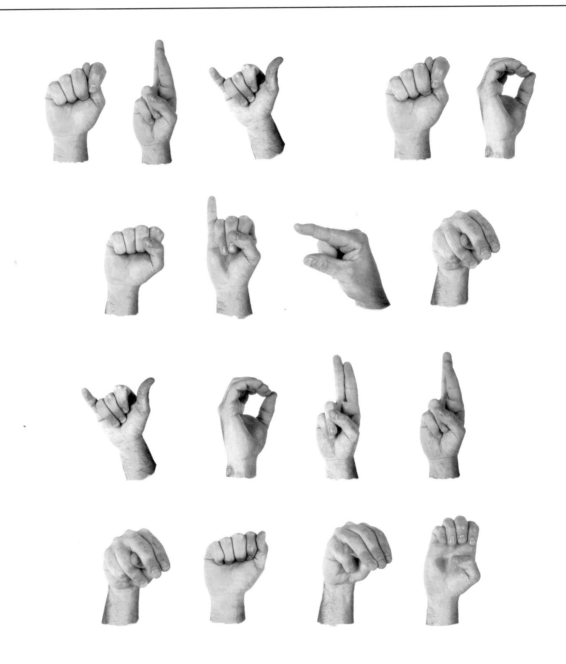

Use the manual alphabet on page 14 to figure out this message. The answer is on page 45.

Chapter 3

The History of Sign Language

"Tag, you're it!" The group of children laughed as they played and ran on that warm summer day in Connecticut. All, that is, except for nine-year-old Alice Cogswell.

The other children did not play with her. She was deaf and dumb, they said.

The Reverend Thomas Hopkins Gallaudet watched her. The kids were playing in his yard.

He got an idea. Gallaudet walked over to Alice, handing her a flower. She walked with him back to the porch.

Gallaudet playfully put his hat on Alice's head. He grabbed a stick and wrote the letters

A silhouette of Alice Cogswell (top) is shown with her teacher, the Reverend Thomas Hopkins Gallaudet (bottom).

17

Abbé Sicard, a French priest, wrote French sign language books.

H-A-T on the ground. Then he pointed to the hat.

Alice laughed. She tapped her shoes on the steps. She wiggled her fingers. She thought this was a great game. But she did not get it.

For more than an hour, Gallaudet pointed at the letters. He traced his fingers over them. He put the hat on his head, and hers, and back again.

Suddenly Alice grabbed the hat. She pulled it way down over her head. She jumped up and pointed to the hat and the word. She got it.

It was the start of something magical for Alice. It was also the start of something for Gallaudet. He became Alice's teacher.

He had never before tried to teach a deaf child. Alice's father gave Gallaudet a set of French sign language books. They had been written by Abbé Sicard, a priest.

No one really knows when or where sign language started. It might have started with monks in the year 530. They had to promise not to talk. Because they could not talk, they used signs to communicate. These signs were passed down.

Some signs look like the words they are supposed to be. The sign for *baby* is like rocking a baby in your arms. To say *girl*, you make the *A* handshape and slide your thumb from cheek to chin. Girls used to wear bonnets, and this motion shows bonnet strings.

Gallaudet learned some signs and then taught Alice. He also wanted to help others like her.

In April 1815, he spoke to businessmen and teachers about the need for deaf schools. Dressed in a flannel nightgown, Alice was carried into the room by her father.

"How do you feel about learning words?" Gallaudet asked her.

She pointed to herself and signed, *I always want to understand.*

The money poured in for a school. Gallaudet took a trip to Europe to learn how

Laurent Clerc helped Gallaudet learn sign language.

The American School for the Deaf, originally called the Connecticut Asylum for the Education and Instruction of Deaf and Dumb Persons, opened over one hundred eighty years ago.

to teach the deaf. He met a young deaf Frenchman who agreed to help. Laurent Clerc, a teacher, came back to America with him.

The Connecticut Asylum for the Education and Instruction of Deaf and Dumb Persons opened on April 15, 1817. It taught health and manners as well as sign language.

Some of the students came from a place where there were a lot of deaf people. The place was Martha's Vineyard. It is a small

island off the coast of Massachusetts. In this place, babies grew up learning sign language. It did not matter if people could hear or not. So many people were deaf in Martha's Vineyard that people had to know how to sign.

Martha's Vineyard was unusual. People who settled there in the eighteenth century had some deaf children. No one really left the island. Everyone married each other. In one

part of the island, one in every four babies born was deaf.

The people on the island made up their own sign language. When the students from the island came to the mainland for school, they shared those signs.

The school used French sign language. There were some new signs, too. This language, and signs that other schools used and shared, would become ASL.

By about 1850, there were schools for deaf students in twelve

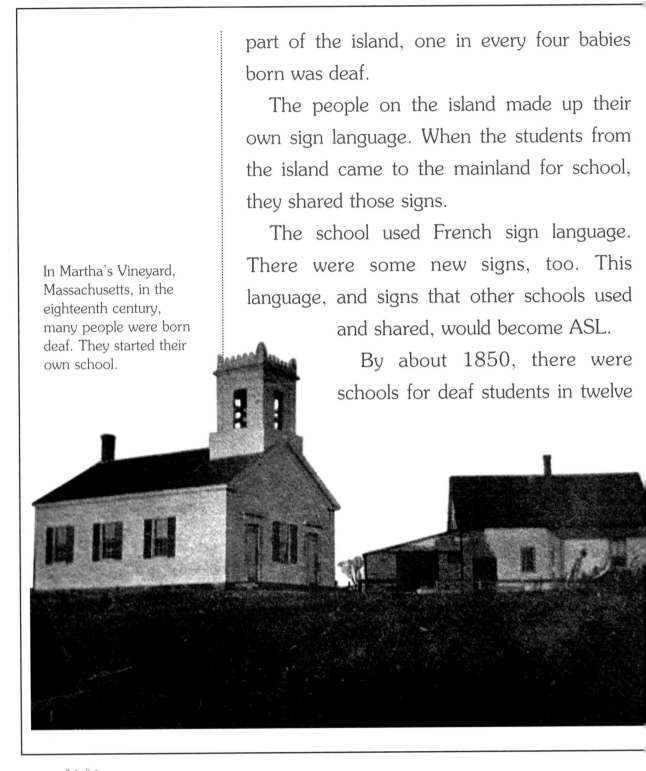

In Martha's Vineyard, Massachusetts, in the eighteenth century, many people were born deaf. They started their own school.

states. By 1864, there was even a college, run by Gallaudet's son, in Washington, D.C. President Abraham Lincoln and Congress created a law for the college. It let deaf students earn college degrees. The college was called the National Deaf-Mute College. In 1986 its name was changed to Gallaudet University.

Abraham Lincoln and Congress created a law in 1864 for a college for deaf students.

In the late 1800s, in England and Scotland, teachers were teaching deaf students by speaking to them. The students could not hear, but they learned to read lips. Some also learned to speak.

It was tried in America. People talked over which way was better, using sign language or speech.

By the early 1900s, teachers of the time thought sign language was not useful. They said it did not let deaf people be part of the hearing environment. So sign language was forbidden.

Sign language was once forbidden and was not taught in schools. But today, sign language has come into its own. Children help each other with signs.

But ASL was still used. The students used it at home with their parents. They used it while playing sports. They used it after school or in the bathrooms. Sometimes they got in trouble for using it, but they kept on doing it.

It went on like this until the 1960s. It was found that using sign language did not slow down speech. It was also found that teaching

just with speech was not the best way. So sign language was used again.

American Sign Language had come into its own. Teachers were needed. Posters and bumper stickers displayed signs. Public places started offering interpreters who could sign.

This teacher uses sign language to teach her class.

An interpreter listens to someone speak. The interpreter then repeats the same phrase in sign language to a deaf person. It can also be done the other way, where a deaf person signs first. The interpreter then speaks the phrase.

Today, you may see someone signing—whether he or she is deaf or not. In the deaf community, it is the language a person chooses to use.

People Who Sign

These are rooftops in Paris.

The five-year-old did not understand what was happening. He had left the only home he knew. Surrounding him now were big buildings, lots of people, and strange smells. The city was Paris and the year 1674. The boy was Etienne de Fay. That day he would be taken to the place where he would live the rest of his life.

At a time when deaf people did only simple jobs, Etienne did great things. He learned sign language. He became an architect. He worked as a sculptor. He was also a librarian and a teacher of deaf children.

Abbé Charles Michel de l'Epée (left) started many deaf schools in Europe.

It would take almost another hundred years for people to understand that deaf people could learn. Sign language played a big role.

About a hundred years later, fifteen-year-old twins lived with their mother in a poor part of Paris. One day, their mother left the girls as they sat at the table sewing, their heads hanging down.

Because they were deaf, they did not hear anyone enter. Abbé Charles Michel de l'Epée was there to help the family learn about God. He wanted to teach the sisters.

He studied the manual language of the sisters. He taught them signs he had seen other deaf people use. This language became a version of French sign language.

Abbé l'Epée helped to start deaf schools in Europe before he died. His work was continued by Abbé Roche-Ambroise Sicard.

Abbé Sicard wrote the books that would get to America. These were the sign language books that the Reverend Thomas Hopkins Gallaudet used to teach Alice Cogswell.

Gallaudet was very smart. He entered Yale University when he was just fourteen. He graduated at the top of his class.

He was also very sick. The oldest of eight children, Gallaudet could not work or play as hard as the others. His chest would burn. He could not breathe. He worried that this would keep him from doing something great with his life.

Gallaudet went to Yale University.

Perhaps Gallaudet's greatest helper was another teacher. This teacher, Laurent Clerc, was deaf himself. When he was twelve, Laurent was sent to Abbé Sicard's school. He stayed on as a teacher after he graduated.

Clerc became good friends with Gallaudet

at this school. Gallaudet asked Clerc to come with him to America to help start a new school for the deaf. During the trip, Gallaudet taught Clerc English. Clerc taught Gallaudet more sign language.

Over the years, there have been many other people known for using sign language. Some were deaf and some were not.

One person who was not deaf was very important to sign language. His name was

In 1897, Gallaudet University looked like this. It was then called Gallaudet College.

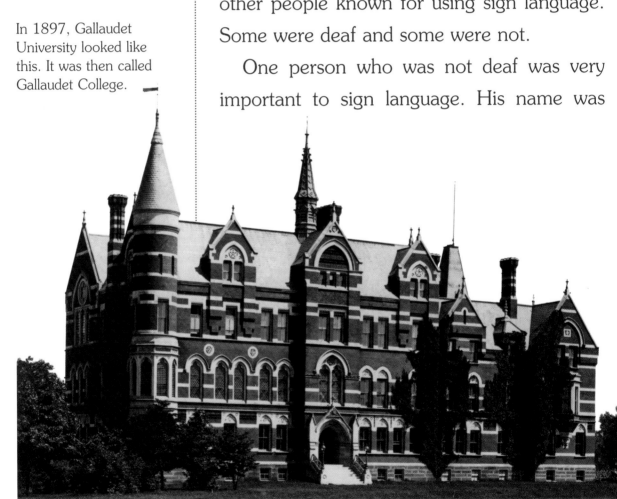

William C. Stokoe, Jr. He was an English teacher at Gallaudet College in the 1950s. When he first saw deaf students signing, he realized something. Sign language was really a language. At the time, most people thought it was just a pantomime—like signals children might use in a game.

Stokoe wrote about what he saw. He proved that American Sign Language was a real language. It had grammar. It had vocabulary. It was put together just like any other language. Stokoe's work changed how people viewed sign language. Signing became more popular than ever.

If you have ever watched *Sesame Street*, you may have seen Linda the Librarian. Linda was played by deaf actress Linda Bove. She used sign language. One of the Muppets would translate so people watching could understand.

Deaf actress Marlee Matlin received

William C. Stokoe, Jr. was a teacher at Gallaudet College in the 1950s. He realized that ASL was a language.

Linda Bove played Linda the Librarian on *Sesame Street*.

worldwide attention for the movie *Children of a Lesser God*. It is a love story about a hearing man and a deaf woman at a deaf school. For her role, which used all sign language except three or four lines, Matlin won the Best Actress Oscar. This is one of the highest awards an actress can win.

Since then, Matlin has appeared on many television shows. She teaches sign language on the children's show *Blue's Clues*. She also has taught it to her daughter who can hear. "She learned to sign when she was 6 months old," said Matlin. "Her first sign was telephone. I called everyone I could think of when she signed that word."

Marlee Matlin signs to a little girl.

Chapter 5

Jobs With Sign Language

One of the first jobs using sign language was teaching in a deaf school. By 1850, teaching had become an important job for deaf people. More than a third of the teachers at deaf schools were deaf themselves. Today, it remains an important job for deaf, hard of hearing, and hearing people.

People who are social workers, ministers, priests, teachers, tour guides, court clerks, or medical office workers can learn sign language to help them in their jobs.

Another job is interpreting. Just knowing sign language does not make someone a

Teachers and students use sign language to learn.

On the opposite page, interpreter Jeff Hardison (left) is interpreting what Senator Robert Dole is saying.

good interpreter. It takes years of study. The Registry of Interpreters for the Deaf is a good resource to check on what is needed.

Sign language can also be used in acting. There are several deaf theater groups that use sign language.

The National Theatre of the Deaf uses sign languages in its performances.

The first was the National Theatre of the Deaf. It opened in 1967 to quite a stir. The actors performed in sign language. Some actors also spoke. They said it was "exciting, inventive, beautiful, and unusual."

It was the first time sign language was used so much in theater. Before, deaf theater groups usually acted out stories. Soon sign language began to be used on television, too. Speeches were translated into sign. Some television shows had deaf characters who signed.

Learning sign language helps many people in their jobs—no matter what type of job they do.

Sign language can now be seen on stage and on TV.

Chapter 6

The Future of Sign Language

FUTURE

Hold your hand up and make the *B* handshape. Move it forward. You have just signed *future*.

The future of sign language looks good. But not all deaf children are learning to sign as early as they should be. Sign language can help them communicate better with others.

Look around and you will see sign language in many different places. One place is the Internet. There are sign language Web sites that show how to sign words. Sometimes this is done with pictures. Sometimes it is done with video.

Technology is helping everyone communicate. This class (left) is communicating with another class using a special video and telephone system. They can sign, and the other class can see them.

Technology could play a great role in the future of sign language. Computers can already recognize speech. People are working to see if they can get computers to recognize hand movements. It might be possible for a computer to translate ASL to English and back again.

Sign language was once taught mostly to deaf people. Now sign language classes are filling up everywhere. Many schools and universities offer ASL as a foreign language.

"Everything that can be expressed in English can be expressed in ASL," said a deaf professor at George Washington University in Washington, D.C.

Videophones can help people who are deaf or hard of hearing communicate with others.

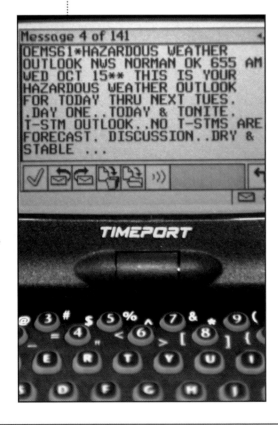

This special pager can help deaf or hard of hearing people. It tells about any strong storms, like tornadoes, that might be heading their way.

"They can understand the world through ASL the way that you understand it through English."

Sign language continues to be taught to many people who can hear. Hearing and deaf people will be able to communicate better. How can sign language help you?

Sign language is used in classrooms. This deaf student watches his interpreter. The interpreter is signing what the teacher is saying.

41

Timeline

1755—Charles Michel Abbé de l'Epée starts the world's first free school for deaf students in Paris, France.

1812—The first public deaf school in America opens in Cobbs, Virginia.

1817—Thomas Gallaudet and Laurent Clerc open the Connecticut Asylum for the Education and Instruction of Deaf and Dumb Persons, the first permanent deaf school in America.

1864—National Deaf-Mute College in Washington, D.C., begins by Congressional decree.

1894—National Deaf-Mute College is renamed Gallaudet College in honor of Thomas Hopkins Gallaudet.

1880s to early 1900s—Sign language is strictly forbidden in many deaf schools.

1965—William C. Stokoe, Jr. publishes the *Dictionary of American Sign Language*.

Timeline

1967—National Theatre of the Deaf is founded in Waterford, Connecticut, and begins touring.

1986—Gallaudet College becomes Gallaudet University.

1988—The historic Deaf President Now (DPN) movement takes place at Gallaudet University. Students and faculty wanted a deaf person to run the university.

1989—Deaf Way, the first international conference and festival, is held at Gallaudet University to celebrate the deaf experience.

1990—Congress passes the Americans with Disabilities Act to help differently abled people.

1997—Congress passes the Individuals with Disabilities Education Act (IDEA) Amendments so schools can better help differently abled children.

Words to Know

American Sign Language (ASL)—The American form of sign language.

environment—Surroundings.

fingerspelling—Using one's fingers to form handshapes in order to spell words.

foreign language—A language other than the one first learned; also sometimes called a second language.

handshape—The position of one's hand when signing or spelling a word.

lipreading—Watching someone's lips to understand the words they are saying.

interpreter—Someone who translates from one language to another, such as from American Sign Language to English.

manual—Relating to the hands.

manual alphabet—The alphabet in finger shapes.

Answer to
Secret Message

T R Y   T O

S I G N

Y O U R

N A M E

Learn More About
Sign Language

Books

Ellerbusch, Kristin. *Talk with Your Hands, Listen with Your Eyes*. Chanhassen, Mich.: Child's World, 1993.

Hafer, Jan C., Robert M. Wilson, and Paul Setzer. *Come Sign With Us*. Washington, D.C.: Gallaudet University Press, June 1996.

Kramer, Jackie, Tali Ovadia, and John Smith (illustrator). *You Can Learn Sign Language: More Than 300 Words in Pictures*. Mahwah, N.J.: Troll Associates, April 2000.

Warner, Penny. *Learn to Sign the Fun Way: Let Your Fingers Do the Talking with Games, Puzzles, and Activities in American Sign Language*. Roseville, Calif.: Prima Publishing, April 2001.

Learn Even More

Videos

I Want to Learn Sign Language, Volumes I and II; American Production Services, 2001.

Talking Hands: A Sign Language Video for Children, Small Fry Productions, 2000.

Internet Addresses

American Sign Language Browser

<http://commtechlab.msu.edu/sites/aslweb/browser.htm>

Pick a word and watch how it is signed.

Counting on Numbers in Sign Language

<http://www.dummies.com/WileyCDA/DummiesArticle/id-1972.html>

Learn more about counting and numbers at this site.

Fingerspelling

<http://where.com/scott.net/asl>

See what words look like when they are fingerspelled.

Index